# CAREER AS A LIVESTOCK BREEDER

ONE OF THE MOST INTERESTING careers today is livestock breeding. Breeders assist with reproduction for such animals as cattle, pigs, sheep and goats. They strive to improve favorable characteristics of these animals (such as higher milk production) by selectively breeding livestock to produce offspring with more desirable traits. Breeders may work on a family-owned ranch, at a large agribusiness facility, or as a self-employed consultant helping farms of all sizes with their breeding programs.

Livestock breeders work in all 50 states, in rural areas, and in or near cities of all sizes. Since agriculture is a highly localized profession – different types of animals are highly dependent on local weather conditions, for example – opportunities are everywhere.

Livestock breeding is a part of the animal science industry. Animal husbandry or animal science refers to breeding livestock and taking care of them from conception throughout adulthood. An animal breeder is someone who works with various types of animals to produce offspring with certain traits (such as faster speed in racehorses). The more specific role of "livestock breeder" refers to someone who breeds agricultural animals (as opposed to exotic animals or household pets like cats and dogs). Breeders are trained in special techniques such as artificial insemination and embryo transference that supplement the natural reproduction of animals.

While you can start a career as a breeder with only a high school diploma and some experience in the field, most positions require at least a two-year associate or four-year undergraduate degree. A graduate degree is often required for the top openings and upper management positions. Breeders can also expect continuing training to stay current with the latest breakthroughs in the field.

The number of livestock breeding jobs is limited and little growth is expected for the foreseeable future. However, demand is expected to remain steady as current breeders retire and new positions open up in agribusiness. Breeding professionals are also needed to help farmers produce healthy livestock with desirable characteristics on a cost-effective basis.

Would livestock breeding be a good fit for you? Having an affinity for animals is paramount, as breeders must have a genuine concern for the health and welfare of the stock in their care. Mathematical and scientific skills are required, as breeding calls for thorough knowledge of genetics and animal biology, plus statistical monitoring of results and trends. An analytical mind and attention to details are needed to select the best animals for breeding and predict the results. Technical training and aptitude are required. Personal traits are also important for success. Do you like helping others – farmers and ranchers, as well as animals? Do you communicate well speaking and in writing? Can you keep pace with newly-discovered information, innovative techniques and regulatory updates? Are you proficient with computers?

If you have good analytical, interpersonal, and technical skills, you can enjoy a long and fulfilling career as a livestock breeder. You will work long hours during breeding seasons, laboring outdoors in all types of weather as you help deliver baby animals and care for adults. However, the satisfaction of caring for animals, solving problems, and helping ranchers increase their profitability makes this a most satisfying career for many breeders.

## WHAT YOU CAN DO NOW

IF YOU ARE CONSIDERING A CAREER AS a livestock breeder, there are several steps you can take while you are still in school to prepare for the profession. Mathematics and science are important core classes, plus there are several electives that can help pave the way. These include anatomy, physiology, animal science, statistics, and computer fundamentals. (Yes, even livestock breeders use computers!) If your school does not offer these electives, you may be able to find courses at a local college or online.

Talk with your school counselor. Counselors can share information about available classes, internships, field trips, part-time work and job shadowing opportunities that can provide valuable insights and experiences.

Learn more about the profession by reading industry publications, many of which can be found online. Visit the websites of the US Department of Agriculture (USDA), and professional organizations such as the National Association of Animal Breeders. Some groups (such as The Livestock Conservancy) offer student memberships.

Get involved with local organizations oriented toward young agricultural professionals, such as Future Farmers of America and 4-H. Attend chapter meetings and decide whether you would like to join. These groups can also help you meet adults who are already employed in agricultural settings. Networking through these organizations helps you learn about scholarships, internships, and entry-level job openings in your region.

Find someone who works as a livestock breeder or with those breeders, such as your county agricultural extension agent. Spending an hour talking one-on-one with a working professional can give you a better perspective on the ups and downs of the day-to-day work. You can find breeders through family contacts, industry associations, your high school guidance counselor, and online searches.

# HISTORY OF THE CAREER

"LIVESTOCK" LITERALLY MEANS LIVING stock, a term that dates back to the Middle Ages, when a person's possessions included both "live" stock and inanimate property (such as land and homes). Today the term refers to animals raised in an agricultural setting for commercial purposes. Livestock includes dairy and beef cattle, swine, sheep, horses, llamas, goats, mules, donkeys, and rabbits. Some definitions also include chickens, ducks and other poultry, and even fish raised on aquaculture farms.

Animal husbandry – breeding and raising livestock – began more than 10,000 years ago when people first began domesticating wild animal species. Goats and sheep were domesticated in Asia around 8,000 BC, with pigs tamed a thousand years later in China and the Middle East. Horses followed around 4,000 BC.

Centuries before genetics emerged as a science, owners realized they could selectively breed certain animals to produce offspring with more favorable observable traits. This was typically accomplished by pairing together male and female animals with desirable traits and allowing them to mate naturally. However, as early as the 14th century, Arabs developed techniques to artificially inseminate female horses to produce colts.

The modern scientific approach to animal breeding was first developed in Europe in the 18th century. Robert Bakewell, a British agriculturist, is considered the founder of systematized selective livestock breeding. Bakewell was the first to stress the need for accurate breeding records. He applied inbreeding techniques to stabilize preferred traits in the offspring, and introduced progeny testing to help breeders evaluate the potential contributions of young sires. Some of these were not new ideas – the Romans suggested progeny testing and observed breeding traits – but Bakewell was the first to take a systematic approach to breeding stock and recording pedigrees. His work led directly to such major British breeds as Dishley Longhorn cattle, New Leicester sheep and the Shire horse.

Bakewell's emphasis on recording pedigrees inspired "herd books" – records listing the lineage of livestock. The first herd book in 1791 listed the pedigrees of horses that had won major races. Other herd books followed for short horn cattle (1822), stud horses (1826), and swine (1876). These records became the basis for the subsequent trend towards "pure breeding," which emphasized improving a breed by mating the best animals within the same breed. While purebreds remain popular today for certain animals (such as dogs and horses), breeders realized most livestock could be better improved by cross-breeding – selectively combining animals from different breeds to produce offspring with the most desirable traits of both parents. Around the same time, the indigenous breeding theory arose in Norway, which held that the best animals were natives to a given area.

The success of Bakewell's techniques drew a number of prominent European disciples who imitated his work and expanded his methods to improve their livestock herds. Bakewell's work also influenced Charles Darwin, who described selective breeding as "artificial selection" in contrast with "natural selection" occurring in the wild.

During the 1800s, as European colonization of the world was at its height, their livestock breeds and techniques spread to new countries. This crossbreeding produced new types of animals better suited to local conditions. The popularity of the breeds produced by

Bakewell and his protégés created a sizeable industry in selling British breeding stock to foreign markets.

Those methods also produced a number of animal breeds that remain popular in the 21st century. For example, the American Angus breed originated in 1873 when British immigrant George Grant brought four Angus bulls from Scotland to Kansas. Shorthorn cattle dominated the United States at that time, so the solid Black Angus cattle without horns (known as "polled," meaning naturally hornless) were unique. Grant crossed his Angus bulls with Texas longhorn cows, producing polled black calves that grew during the winter and weighed more in the springtime. Today the American Angus Association "records more cattle each year than any other beef breed association, making it the largest beef breed registry in the world," the group reports.

By the early 20th century, the science of genetics began influencing animal breeding techniques. In 1865, Gregor Mendel published his studies on genetics, but it took decades before that work led to broad application of those principles. By 1925, the United States government's newly-established network of agricultural experiment stations began comparing how different breeds performed in different parts of the country. That work led to formalized herd management principles, performance testing in herds, and the trend of selecting breeding animals on the basis of genetic superiority.

The first successful embryo transfer took place in the 1890s, when Walter Heap of England transferred embryos from pregnant rabbits into other females. However, the practice was not used commercially in the cattle industry until the mid-20th century, when hormones became available that made transfers practical on a larger scale.

Today, breeders transfer embryos from top female animals into lower-quality surrogates. These surrogate mothers deliver the transplanted young while the higher-quality donor mother is available to be impregnated again. The technique allows more offspring to be produced by the highest quality animals, improving production and upgrading the genetic strain of the herd.

Over the past 150 years, livestock breeders have dramatically increased the health, profitability and food production of agricultural animals. However, with the emphasis on commercially-viable breeds of cattle and pigs, hundreds of other less-profitable breeds have become extinct. The sustainable farming movement in recent years has focused attention on heritage livestock – breeds that were previously raised naturally by small farmers before agriculture became industrialized. Groups such as The Livestock Conservancy are working to preserve and expand populations of the remaining heritage animals.

## WHERE YOU WILL WORK

MOST LIVESTOCK BREEDERS WORK ON farms in rural parts of the country, with livestock farms found in all 50 states. According to government statistics, Kentucky is the state with the largest employment of animal breeders (a career category that includes both livestock and pet breeders). Wisconsin ranks second, followed by California, Iowa and New York.

Michigan ranks as the top paying state for breeders (almost $55,000 annually), followed by Wisconsin, California, New York and Indiana.

Lexington, Kentucky is the metropolitan area with the highest number of breeders, followed by Modesto, California, and Madison, Wisconsin.

The vast majority of breeders work in the animal production industry. Animal slaughtering and processing is the second largest employer, followed by scientific research and development services. The scientific research industry is the highest-paying group, followed by animal production.

Breeders may be employees of a farm, agribusiness or another company, or they may be self-employed. Breeders select animals for breeding to produce offspring with desirable characteristics, as well as facilitate reproduction through natural or artificial means. Employed breeders also take care of animals, including overseeing animal births, monitoring their health, and providing basic medical care. Breeders are not usually veterinarians, but they typically have some animal medical training and work with veterinarians on health issues.

Many other breeders are self-employed contractors who work for several clients, traveling from one farm to another to help individual facilities devise and execute breeding programs. Contractor breeders are not normally as involved in the daily care of animals as an employee would be. They may work with farm staff on animal breeding and care, or they may supervise their own employees who work at a particular facility. Contractors have more job flexibility and can earn more money, but they must also run a business in addition to spending long hours on the many tasks associated with breeding animals. They must be on the farm during breeding season, and may also be required to be available during birthing.

Both employee and contractor breeders typically specialize in one type of livestock, such as cattle or sheep. Some specialize even further. For example, some quarter horse breeders focus on animals that are bred for specific halter show classes, while others concentrate on producing fast horses that win races. Other breeders may specialize just in producing animals with certain traits, such as stamina for farm work, or meat production rather than milk production in cattle.

Breeders can also work in non-farm settings. They may work in offices, laboratories, or research centers for agribusiness corporations, such as those that manufacture artificial insemination equipment and medications. Veterinarians can also work outside their practice as livestock breeders. Other breeders teach agriculture, genetics and animal husbandry at high schools, colleges and universities across the country.

## THE WORK YOU WILL DO

WHILE MOST LIVESTOCK BREEDERS work on ranches and farms, a career in this industry can provide more versatile opportunities than you might expect. You could become an entrepreneur, running your own business while helping others breed their animals for optimal results. You might also manage a breeding operation for an agribusiness company, help government regulators inspect livestock operations, sell breeding equipment and supplies, or teach others how to become a breeder.

The majority of breeders work on farms and ranches. Most are self-employed, providing services to several clients on a contract basis. Some breeders work in the profession part time during peak seasons and have other full-time jobs that provide the majority of their income. However, larger ranches and agricultural operations may employ their own breeders who also take care of the animals.

As a livestock breeder, there are many animals you could work with: cattle, pigs, sheep, goats, llamas, mules, poultry, horses – practically any creature raised on a farm or ranch for commercial purposes. Breeders typically focus on one type of animal (such as cattle), and sometimes specialize just in advancing certain traits (such as increased milk production from cows or hogs that can grow to market weight faster). Each type of animal requires specialized expertise, so most breeders find concentrating in a certain specialty brings better results and enhances their own value in the marketplace.

Breeders work to improve specific characteristics in the animals they work with. They spend considerable time and energy researching the characteristics of potential parents. They consider such factors as ancestry, health, behavior, weight, size and genetic traits. This analysis helps them decide which combinations of mothers and sires are likely to produce offspring with the desired traits. While there is considerable science involved in genetic selection, breeders also must experiment at times with new combinations to see what the results will be. Years of experience help breeders hone their skills and instincts as they plan for future reproductive projects.

Depending upon the situation, breeders may work to encourage conventional mating of selected animals, or they may use artificial techniques. "Live cover" breeding refers to the typical natural situation where a male and female animal are brought together to mate. One form of live cover is pasture breeding, where the animals are left on their own to mate. They may live together outdoors, or come together for a short period of time when the female is in heat. However, the success rate for achieving pregnancy is typically higher for hand breeding, in which the breeder actively guides the mating process.

Artificial methods include artificial insemination (AI) of the female, and embryo transfer. The latter technique calls for extracting an embryo from a high-quality mother and transferring it to a lesser-quality female who will carry it through gestation. This method allows the original mother to return to the breeding pool more quickly, and uses the less desirable surrogate mother to deliver a more desirable child than it would have otherwise produced on its own.

Some breeders work as technicians who collect, package and label containers of semen for AI applications. The semen is examined with a microscope to ensure that the quality is acceptable. It is then frozen and stored for later use, when it will be injected into females through calibrated syringes and inseminating guns. These containers may be used at the originating ranch, or sold to other farms. As with other methods, the breeder keeps detailed records on the success of these techniques in order to evaluate both the male and female animals, and to determine the effectiveness of natural (stud) procedures versus AI techniques.

The discipline of livestock breeding requires professionals to keep a great number of records. They review the pedigrees of animals in records either kept on the farm or listed with national registries (such as those from the American Angus Association or the National Registry of Swine). Breeders also track the results of their own work, noting which animals were bred, which traits were passed on to their offspring, and how the youngsters performed. They record each individual animal's rates of growth, how much food it eats and what kind, what illnesses it has and what medication it is given, and the general success of their breeding work. On many ranches, these records are kept in computer databases, while others maintain data on handwritten paper documents.

Breeders put in long hours and their work is physically demanding. Taking care of animals is a full-time job that can last around the clock and throughout the year. Breeders are particularly busy at times when the females in the herd are in heat, and during the birthing seasons. They may be involved in helping deliver the offspring, as well as feeding and watering the animals. Breeders examine animals for signs of injury or illness. They may treat these animals themselves for minor illnesses, or they make work with a veterinarian for conditions that are more urgent and on vaccination programs.

In their normal course of duties, breeders draw on their knowledge of animal species, genealogy, genetics and individual traits to select the animals with the highest probability for passing on desirable traits to their offspring. Some breeders supervise others who take care of individual animals. Others (particularly those employed by a single farm or company) may also serve as caretakers, feeding and watering cattle, cleaning pig pens, or shearing sheep. Breeders are also involved in branding, tagging or tattooing animals for identification under the breeding program.

Breeders may work on one farm or travel between several ranches. In some cases, breeders also sell the animals they raise at auctions, or on the open market. They may also show their animals at livestock shows, where they compete for awards that help them attract buyers. They may sell animals directly to small ranches or research centers. These breeders also must monitor market prices to ensure they get the proper return on their sales.

A person working as a livestock breeder may be called by several different titles. Those include animal husbandman, artificial insemination (AI) technician, livestock rancher, chicken fancier, animal technician, or poultry inseminator. Those in management positions may be known as breeding manager, broodmare foreman or stallion manager.

Breeders who are self-employed also have additional duties beyond breeding animals. They are running their own business, so they must track income and expenses, file regular financial reports, and comply with the same tax regulations that accompany any small enterprise. If they have employees, they must also fund their payroll and file additional regulatory documents with state and federal authorities. They must also continually market their services to potential new clients. Independent breeders who specialize in certain species must meet the standards and regulations of the professional societies that oversee those animals. Certified breeders can then advertise that their animals are pedigreed, thoroughbreds, purebreds, or otherwise approved by the national association.

An animal husbandry or animal science degree can also prepare you for a number of other roles. You may move up into management, leading teams of other breeders. You might become a judge at an animal show or take a position with a breeding association. You may move into agricultural research, working, for example, as a dairy scientist who not only breeds cows, but also makes sure their nutritional needs are met and keeps the milk supply safe. Others work with agribusiness companies that make nutritional supplements, artificial insemination equipment, and other products aimed at the breeding industry. They may also work for government regulators, at agricultural inspection facilities, or at experiment stations with the USDA Cooperative Extension Service.

Teaching is another option for those working as livestock breeders. Many high schools, vocational and technical schools, colleges, and universities employ agricultural teachers who cover livestock breeding topics. At the high school level, you may be involved with the local chapter of the Future Farmers of America, helping your students raise cows and pigs to compete at the county fair. Every state has at least one land grant college with an agricultural program, so there are opportunities across the country for professors who can educate the next generation of livestock breeders.

## LIFE STORIES OF LIVESTOCK BREEDERS

### I Breed Beef Cattle for Florida Ranches

"When most people think of Florida, they picture sandy beaches, sparkling oceans, sunshine, and amusement parks – but probably not cattle ranches. You may not realize that Florida is one of the top US cattle producers, with more than one million animals. Our breeding herds and calves are valued at more than $1 billion.

I've worked with Florida beef cattle all my life. My family owns a ranch in Central Florida where we breed and raise Brahmans, Angus and other types of beef cattle that do well in the warm, sandy regions of the state. So I grew up tending the herd, doing farm chores, and raising calves for FFA and 4-H competitions. We followed a typical farm schedule, spending long hours working in a rural area of the state – even though we were only an hour from the beaches of the Atlantic Ocean and the major tourist attractions at Orlando!

After high school, I attended the University of Florida, the first land grant college in the state. I knew I wanted to work in agriculture, but I also knew I did not want the headaches and challenges of owning and operating my own ranch. Since I was not really sure what to major in, I studied a variety of agribusiness subjects. Soon I settled on livestock breeding, an area where I could build on my earlier experience raising calves to show at the county fair. I knew a little about natural breeding techniques, because our family ranch used stud services to breed our cows. At college, I learned more about the advantages of artificial insemination (AI), and the latest techniques and equipment to help do the job.

When I graduated from the university, I returned to our farm and put into practice what I had learned about diversifying the herd through artificial insemination. Soon I was sharing AI methods with our neighbors and helping them establish more sophisticated breeding programs.

While I had not started out with the intention of starting my own business, that is exactly what happened! Since we have limited pastures available in Florida, the main focus of the cattle industry is providing calves for export to other states. That means successful livestock breeders are in high demand throughout the cattle producing regions of the state. Soon I started my own livestock breeding company, traveling to ranches and farms in Central Florida to consult with clients. I stay pretty busy during breeding season, and I still work on the family farm when things slow down.

Livestock breeding has also led to a new hobby. In college, I became interested in preserving the historical Florida Cracker Cattle breed that once dominated the state. Like the Texas Longhorns, Florida Cracker Cattle were introduced hundreds of years ago by early Spanish explorers. They once roamed free throughout the state, and were rounded up periodically and herded to market. There are not many offspring of these historic animals left. I am breeding a few on our farm, and working with the Florida Cracker/Pineywoods Breed Association and Registry to help preserve them."

## I Am a Swine Breeder at My Own Organic Farm

"I grew up on a typical family farm in upstate New York. We planted and harvested vegetables, as well as raised pigs and chickens. We took our produce and livestock to the county marketplace every weekend. Our meat and vegetables ended up in restaurants in New York City and on dinner tables throughout New England. Spring, summer and fall were busy times as we tended to crops and brought new animals into the world.

My intention from my earliest days was to remain on the farm and keep it going after my parents handed it down to me. I attended the State University of New York (SUNY) College of Agriculture and Technology at Cobleskill, the top area school for agricultural studies. I pursued a fairly diversified curriculum, as I wanted to learn how to grow better vegetables as well as produce healthy poultry and swine.

Fortunately, while I was in school, the sustainable agriculture movement spilled over into the classroom. The general public wanted more naturally grown foods using fewer chemicals and pesticides. My family was already seeing a decline in our sales as more consumers favored organic farms and grain-fed meats. So in my third year of college, I shifted my focus toward livestock breeding techniques. While raising healthier chickens was often a matter of giving them the right foods, creating 'better pigs' also required the right breeding and bloodlines to produce swine that would thrive on such a diet.

Back on the farm, I became responsible for all our pork operations. I kept records on the pigs, selecting the best breeding combinations, avoiding antibiotics, and making sure our swine were raised according to guidelines that would allow their meat to be certified 'all natural.' At the same time, my sister learned everything she could about growing organic vegetables, and she took over the produce part of our business. We brought sustainable farming practices to our operation and are growing that portion of our business. Our plan is that within two years, we will only be producing organic vegetables and free-range pigs. Soon my parents will retire and turn the farm over to us. My training as a livestock breeder allows me to complete our transition to an all-natural operation and keep the family farm going for the next generation."

## PERSONAL QUALIFICATIONS

BREEDERS NEED TO BE COMPASSIONATE, with a real interest in working to improve the lives of animals – even those who are destined for the marketplace (and the dinner table). Breeders constantly work to increase the world's food supply while protecting its natural resources. Your work in this field will have a positive impact on the animals in your care, as well as on your family, neighbors and people around the world who benefit from a steady, safe, affordable food supply.

If you like learning new skills, identifying issues, and challenging yourself to solve problems, you will enjoy this field. You will combine your knowledge of animals with scientific and mathematical analysis to improve livestock traits. Breeders consider the costs and benefits of different breeding techniques, and use logic to evaluate the strengths and weaknesses of those choices. They also are aware when problems develop, or when they detect that something is likely to go wrong, and they devise solutions. Similarly, if an animal becomes ill and a veterinarian is not available, you need to be able to treat the animal on your own.

Many breeders work on farms of all sizes across the country, although some work for companies located in major metropolitan areas. They spend much of their time taking care of animals, as they evaluate and select the best candidates for breeding. However, whether you are self-employed or work for someone, you also spend time working with other people. You must be willing to share research and work as a team member as you strive towards improvement of a species. You may need to bring others together to discuss different approaches and come to a consensus on the best solution to a problem. If you work in a management role, you will also need to be a good leader who can keep your team motivated, focused, and running smoothly. In addition, if you go to work for yourself, you will need to be able to run your own business, market your services, and manage your time appropriately.

Working with animals demands a calm demeanor and physical stamina to help you cope with the long hours and demanding labor that accompany farm life. Computer software and hardware skills are also important, as automated solutions are generally applied to the extensive record keeping and analysis required for breeding.

You may also be working with machinery, tools, and specialized equipment for such tasks as artificial insemination and embryo transfer. If the machine breaks down and a technician is not available, you may need to repair it yourself, so it helps to be handy with tools and have a knack for fixing things.

Regardless of where you decide to work and what animals you specialize in, a career in livestock breeding can be personally rewarding throughout your lifetime.

## ATTRACTIVE FEATURES

MANY LIVESTOCK BREEDERS REPORT high levels of job satisfaction, with most saying their careers are personally rewarding and fulfilling.

While the number of livestock breeders is expected to remain relatively small, demand for experts who can help farmers, ranchers and companies improve their herds is expected to continue. Regardless of economic cycles over your working years, people will always eat meat, drink milk, and wear clothing made from wool. Livestock breeders enjoy living a rural lifestyle and working with animals.

Breeders are able to help improve livestock herds by combining their knowledge of animal biology and behavior, genetics, mathematics and statistics. They may help produce cows that give more milk, sheep with higher quality wool, or hogs that fatten to market weight sooner. They apply their skills to evaluating the best solution to a given situation, such as determining whether natural breeding or artificial insemination is a better alternative for a particular rancher to increase the quality of the herd.

Livestock breeders may be found on family farms or at agricultural enterprises owned by agribusinesses. Many breeders who have grown up in a rural setting decide to stay on the farm, while others move from the cities to the countryside in pursuit of a more inviting lifestyle. Although there are fewer family farms than in the past, many of those have shifted their attention to sustainable farming and environmentally-friendly methods to care for their animals. The increasing popularity of grain-fed, organically produced beef, poultry and other meats means more opportunities for breeders who can help farmers produce the safest possible food products for customers.

Many breeders are self-employed and prefer "being their own boss," traveling from one farm to another to support breeding programs. They may also travel to shows where they display the animals they breed. Others pursue careers as breeders or breeding managers for larger companies that own and operate consolidated farming operations. These breeders design and administer breeding programs for large farms and ranches, while managers focus on directing employees and making operations more efficient. There are opportunities to "climb the corporate ladder" in agribusiness, so animal breeders can enjoy the amenities of a rural setting while pursuing a management career. Employees also typically receive benefits such as insurance, vacations, and retirement plans.

A variety of livestock breeding professionals work in cities of all sizes across the country. Some work for companies that manufacture products and machinery for the breeding industry, such as artificial insemination equipment. Others work for government agencies that regulate the food industry. There are also breeders working as teachers at colleges, universities and high schools, educating the next generation of livestock professionals. These professionals and others like them are able to apply their affinity with animals and their technical expertise in breeding to help tackle the challenges of feeding the world, compassionately caring for animals, and preserving the natural environment.

## UNATTRACTIVE FEATURES

WHILE A CAREER AS A LIVESTOCK breeder carries many rewards, the work is demanding and stressful. The hours are often long and physically draining — particularly if you work on a farm where your schedule is driven by the needs of the herd. Sometimes you need physical strength to handle an unruly animal. Techniques such as artificial insemination can be complex. Even if you manage a team of workers who do most of the actual labor, you still need to know how to do each job and fill in for absentees on short notice.

While breeders' schedules are driven in part by the mating seasons of the animals they care for, tending to herds and flocks can be a year-around calling. Breeders are often called upon to help with deliveries of calves and colts, for example, and those births may occur at any time of the day or night. The varying ovulation cycles also mean the incomes of animal breeders can change significantly as a function of the seasons and the mating patterns of their herds – particularly for those who are self-employed.

Breeders also face constant demands for education – both to get started in the field and to stay on top of the latest developments in genetics, breeding techniques, and herd management. They must also keep current on government regulations for animal care, which evolve continually. Working with an organic dairy or sustainable beef operation provides additional challenges to make sure farms comply with regulations for certifying organic products.

If you go to work for a larger company, your employer may offer training courses. However, a self-employed breeder or one on a small family farm must find the time and money to pursue those educational opportunities on his or her own. Certifications in specialized areas of breeding can help to advance your career, but you will need time and funds to obtain certifications and keep them renewed.

Breeders spend a good portion of their time keeping records, either through software programs or in paper notebooks. Those who work for large companies face the same challenges as other corporate employees. In addition to unruly animals, they may deal with demanding managers, unhelpful colleagues, personality conflicts, and office politics. Self-employed livestock breeders also deal with unreasonable customers on top of the challenges of running a successful small business.

Some people may not like the slower pace of life and relative isolation that comes from living in a rural agricultural area. Whether self-employed or working directly for an agricultural enterprise, most breeders work on farms and ranches, laboring for long hours outside in all types of weather. Meanwhile, those who work for companies in urban and suburban areas face such issues as overcrowded highways, high living costs, and poor quality of life.

Working on a farm can be hazardous, particularly if you breed large animals. While accidents are not common, there is always a risk of being kicked by a mule or bitten by a goat. Some machinery and equipment can cause serious injuries if you do not follow proper safety precautions. Breeders must also be careful working with chemicals to avoid accidents, keep their herds safe, and prevent environmental damage. When they are not on the farm, breeders (like other professionals who work in office environments) may face health problems that stem from extended stress. Frequent computer use can lead to eyestrain, back pain, and repetitive motion injuries such as carpal tunnel syndrome.

## EDUCATION AND TRAINING

YOU COULD BEGIN A CAREER IN LIVESTOCK breeding with only a high school degree, plus some work experience in a related field (particularly on a farm). Some technical schools and two-year colleges offer associate degrees in animal breeding that would also help you get started in an entry-level position. However, many employers prefer a four-year degree from a college or university, as it indicates that the candidate is up-to-date on current technologies and procedures. A graduate degree is not typically expected, although it can be helpful to land positions that are more advanced. A master's may be required if you move into upper management, teaching, or agricultural research.

Every state has at least one land-grant college that provides higher education in agricultural sciences. In addition, most colleges and universities provide animal husbandry, animal science and similar curriculums. Student enrollment in agricultural programs has reached new highs in recent years. Many colleges and universities have a school of agriculture with experienced professors and a variety of specialization tracks in areas such as animal science and agri-science technology.

Universities also have organizations geared toward agriculture students, such as clubs for students in specialty areas like agribusiness, and fraternities and sororities for agriculture students (such as Alpha Zeta, Alpha Gamma Rho and Sigma Alpha).

For example, the Texas A&M University Department of Animal Science offers courses through its animal breeding and genetics section for undergraduate students, as well as master's and doctoral degrees in animal breeding. The department "works to provide new scientific discoveries to age-old livestock production problems to help producers and consumers," Texas A&M states on its website. "The field of animal breeding and genetics research is more exciting than ever before, with projects such as bovine gene mapping and DNA sequencing." Researchers at the university use "state of the art tools and facilities" as they "contribute to the field of animal biotechnology on a worldwide level."

Major universities also have state-of-the-art computer systems, animal science laboratories, working farms, research stations, and similar centers for agricultural studies. Students may work with local agricultural extension agents, breeders, researchers, ranchers, and agribusinesses through internships, class projects and other programs.

Breeders generally focus their studies on such topics as animal science, genetics, biotechnology, animal husbandry, and biometrics (applying statistical and advanced mathematical analysis to biological data). Many breeders have at least a bachelor's degree in animal science, animal reproduction or biology. Students in animal breeding and animal science courses study applying genetic engineering principles to developing new animal breeds or enhancing existing breeds, improving animals' health, and selectively upgrading animal populations in a farm setting.

One recent ranking of the top 10 US agriculture universities lists:

Michigan State University

Cornell University

University of California-Davis

University of Minnesota

University of Illinois – Urbana-Champaign

Purdue University-West Lafayette

Washington State University

University of Wisconsin

Iowa State University

University of Georgia

Another national ranking lists Utah State, California Polytechnic-San Lois Obispo, Purdue and Montana State University as the four best colleges for agriculture majors.

One ranking of colleges and universities with programs that focus on animal breeding and science includes the State University of New York, University of Nevada-Reno, Lake Erie College in Ohio, Kishwaukee College in Illinois, and Hinds Community College in Mississippi.

With so many choices, how do you pick the right educational institution for you? Start with national rankings of colleges and universities, such as the annual surveys by US News and World Reports. Search for websites that rank the top schools for agriculture. Use these surveys to narrow your options, and then visit the websites of individual schools to learn more. Make sure the universities you consider offer plenty of opportunities for hands-on experience outside the classroom.

After graduation, certifications and licenses may also be required for certain types of positions, to either land your first job or move up in the profession. These certifications vary widely depending upon the types of animals you work with and the type of job you do. For example, the Mississippi Master Cattle Producer Program includes training on breeding and genetics. The Certified Horsemanship Association offers certification for equine facility managers. Most normal farm operations are exempted from USDA license requirements for animal breeders and dealers, but there are some areas that call for a license (such as breeding animals for laboratory use).

In addition to certification classes, expect ongoing training throughout your career. Breeders need to stay up-to-date on the latest techniques and breakthroughs so they can put that knowledge to practical use in their daily work. You can expect to receive periodic training during your career through a variety of formal and informal settings, such as presentations from your local USDA Extension Service agent.

## EARNINGS

ANIMAL BREEDERS (A CATEGORY THAT includes livestock breeders, pet breeders and other types) earn an average annual salary of about $40,000. The top 10 percent of earners make about $60,000, and the bottom 10 percent are paid only about $20,000.

Breeders work in a variety of environments and for a large range of employers, so their earnings vary greatly. They may be paid an hourly wage, an annual salary, or by some other arrangement. Those who work for themselves may receive a higher hourly pay rate than an employee would, but these independent contractors may also go weeks between jobs. Self-employed breeders must also supply their own benefits (such as health insurance), while employees at larger firms receive vacation, insurance and similar benefits as part of their compensation package. Many self-employed breeders also work part time and earn some of their income through other employment.

Breeders who move into management can expect higher salaries. Farmers, ranchers and agricultural managers earn an average of $60,000. The lowest 10 percent earn about $30,000, and the top 10 percent earn more than $100,000.

# OPPORTUNITIES

EMPLOYMENT OF ANIMAL BREEDERS (including breeders of both livestock and non-agricultural animals) is forecast to decline by seven percent over the coming decade. There are about 11,000 people currently working full time in the career, with that number expected to drop to about 10,700 by 2020.

While the number of traditional breeding positions at conventional farms is expected to decline, the overall demand for breeders is expected to remain steady. Job openings throughout the agricultural sector are generally plentiful because many workers leave their positions to pursue new opportunities, move into management, or decide to change careers because of the physical demands of farm life. A number of breeders are also nearing retirement age, which will create opportunities for younger workers to take their places in the work force.

Managers in the breeding profession face a shrinking job market. Employment of farmers, ranchers and other agricultural managers is predicted to decline by about eight percent over the coming decade. The agricultural sector continues to produce more with fewer workers. With the costs of buying and operating a farm rising, more farms may be sold to well-capitalized companies and the land consolidated into larger, more productive farms.

Experts also expect there will be more opportunities for breeders to work in other sectors. Larger livestock operations need breeders, as do companies that supply animals to laboratories and zoos. With the cost of genotyping and genetic sequencing declining, new job opportunities are expected as this research finds common use in livestock management. Breeders are working on practical applications of genetic research in sequencing livestock genomes, DNA-based marker assisted herd management and selection, and similar innovations. The sustainable agriculture movement is also driving demand for experts who can help mitigate the environmental damage done by ecologically unfriendly farming practices. Breeders can also apply their skills to preserving rare and endangered animals by helping expand the shrinking populations of these creatures.

A number of breeders decide to go into business for themselves, particularly if they work part time or specialize in certain types of animals (such as dairy goats or Angus cattle). Self-employment can open up new opportunities that are not available to most employees to learn new skills, travel and expand their network of contacts. However, being your own boss also demands additional skills to run your own business, market your services, and manage your workflow. Opportunities are always out there for entrepreneurs, but they also carry risks which make it difficult to predict how many people would be able to make the transition to being a self-employed breeder.

## GETTING STARTED

DOES A CAREER AS A LIVESTOCK breeder seem like a good fit for you? Choosing your future career is a vital first step, but it is only one step. There is no time like your high school years to start preparing for the future.

Begin by gathering more detailed information about livestock breeding. Do you have a specific type of animal you want to work with — cattle, sheep, pigs, goats or exotic breeds? Do you want to work on a small family farm, with a large agribusiness, or for another type of corporation? Research your options through books, magazines, websites and similar sources of information. Information is available online, at your local library, from colleges and universities, and through your high school guidance counselors. Check local newspapers and industry trade magazines to learn about job openings, internships, industry events, meetings, and volunteer opportunities.

Many employers require at least a four-year degree in animal husbandry, agricultural science or a similar major to get started, although you can land an entry-level position with a two-year associate degree. Higher-level positions (such as top management) often require a graduate degree. Every state has at least one land-grant college or university that offers degrees in animal science and related topics. In addition to land grant schools, many other colleges, universities and private institutions offer an agricultural curriculum. Set aside a significant amount of time for research and campus visits to determine which school will provide the best training for your goals.

In addition to formal training, think about how you could gain some working experience to enhance your résumé — and maybe earn some extra money. Investigate whether there are internships, volunteer opportunities or work-study programs available at or near the school you plan to attend. You may be able to find an entry-level position on a part-time basis (or a full-time summer job) in the agricultural field, preferably working directly with breeders.

Talk to breeders (or your local extension agent) about your goals. Ask what personal traits and training programs they believe are the most important to building a successful career. Are there industry organizations where you can attend local sessions and meet others in the profession? Many groups have outreach programs that specifically target agricultural students.

Discuss your plans with family and friends. Ask whether they believe a career in animal breeding would be a good choice for you. Meet with your high school guidance counselors to discuss your plans and gain their insights. Your counselor can also share information about helpful opportunities in your region.

Once you gather the information, it is time to review your data and weigh your options. Does livestock breeding still feel like a sound choice for the future? Do you have the right skills – an affinity for animals, good math and science grades, an analytical mind and a passion for working outdoors? The bottom line is: can you see yourself enjoying a career as a livestock breeder? If the answer is yes, take those first steps today toward an interesting new career!

## ASSOCIATIONS

American Angus Association
http://www.angus.org

American Dairy Goat Association
http://www.adga.org

American Farm Bureau Federation
http://www.fb.org

American Livestock Breeds Conservancy
www.albc-usa.org

American Sheep Industry Association
http://www.sheepusa.org

American Society of Farm Managers and
Agricultural Appraisers
http://www.asfmra.org

Certified Horsemanship Association
http://www.cha-ahse.org

Future Farmers of America
https://www.ffa.org

Livestock Conservancy
www.livestockconservancy.org

National Association of Animal Breeders
http://www.naab-css.org

National Swine Registry
http://www.nationalswine.com

4-H Youth Development
http://www.4-h.org


# PERIODICALS

Agrolook Magazine
www.agrolook.com

American Brahman Review
www.brahmanreview.com

American Cattlemen Magazine
www.americancattlemen.com

Angus Journal
www.angusproductions.com

Beef Magazine/Breeding
www.beefmagazine.com

Dairy Management
http://www.dairyinfo.com

Farming Magazine
www.farmingmagazine.net

Journal of Sustainable Agriculture
http://www.tandfonline.com

Livestock Science
http://www.sciencedirect.com

Profitable Pig Production
www.profitablepigproduction.com

Progressive Dairyman
www.progressivedairy.com

Progressive Farmer
www.dtnprogressivefarmer.com/dtnag

Southern Livestock Standard
www.southernlivestock.com

## WEBSITES

AgCareers
http://www.agcareers.com

Breeders' World
http://www.breedersworld.com

Cattle Today
http://www.cattletoday.com

Dairy Farming Today
http://www.dairyfarmingtoday.org

Farm Service Agency
http://www.fsa.usda.gov

Master Cattle Producer Program
http://msucares.com/livestock/beef/mcp

National Hog Farmer
http://www.nationalhogfarmer.com

Pig Progress
www.pigprogress.com

National Agricultural Library
http://www.nal.usda.gov

National Institute of Food and Agriculture
http://www.nifa.usda.gov

US Department of Agriculture
http://www.usda.gov

xTension (USDA Cooperative Extension System)
http://www.extension.org

www.ingramcontent.com/pod-product-compliance
Lightning Source LLC
Chambersburg PA
CBHW070521290526
45790CB00003B/1264